50 Premium Homemade Pizza Dishes

By: Kelly Johnson

Table of Contents

- Margherita Pizza
- Pepperoni Pizza
- Quattro Stagioni Pizza
- BBQ Chicken Pizza
- Prosciutto and Arugula Pizza
- Veggie Supreme Pizza
- Hawaiian Pizza
- White Garlic Chicken Pizza
- Margherita with Balsamic Glaze
- Spicy Italian Sausage Pizza
- Mushroom and Truffle Oil Pizza
- Four Cheese Pizza (Quattro Formaggi)
- Shrimp Scampi Pizza
- Pesto Chicken Pizza
- Buffalo Chicken Pizza
- Fig and Prosciutto Pizza
- Spinach and Ricotta Pizza
- Meat Lovers Pizza
- Caprese Pizza
- Eggplant Parmesan Pizza
- Clam Pizza
- Roasted Red Pepper and Goat Cheese Pizza
- Sausage and Peppers Pizza
- Mediterranean Pizza (Olives, Feta, and Spinach)
- Mexican Street Corn Pizza
- BBQ Pulled Pork Pizza
- Smoked Salmon and Cream Cheese Pizza
- Breakfast Pizza (Eggs and Bacon)
- Beef and Blue Cheese Pizza
- Peppadew and Ricotta Pizza
- Pear and Gorgonzola Pizza
- Mushroom and Bacon Pizza
- Chicken Alfredo Pizza
- Zaatar and Feta Pizza
- Black Olive and Anchovy Pizza

- White Pizzaiola (Tomato-Free Pizza)
- Spicy Tuna Pizza
- Margherita with Burrata
- Shrimp and Pesto Pizza
- Caramelized Onion and Goat Cheese Pizza
- Artichoke and Parmesan Pizza
- Chorizo and Sweet Potato Pizza
- Bacon and Brussels Sprouts Pizza
- Italian Sausage and Ricotta Pizza
- Roasted Beet and Arugula Pizza
- Wild Mushroom and Thyme Pizza
- Roasted Garlic and Tomato Pizza
- Sweet and Sour Pork Pizza
- Butternut Squash and Sage Pizza
- Grilled Vegetable Pizza

Margherita Pizza

Ingredients:

- 1 pizza dough
- 1/2 cup tomato sauce
- 8 oz fresh mozzarella cheese, sliced
- Fresh basil leaves
- Olive oil
- Salt to taste

Instructions:

1. Preheat the oven to 475°F (245°C).
2. Roll out the pizza dough to your desired thickness and place it on a baking sheet or pizza stone.
3. Spread the tomato sauce evenly on the dough.
4. Top with fresh mozzarella cheese slices.
5. Bake for 10-12 minutes until the crust is golden and the cheese is melted.
6. Remove from the oven and top with fresh basil leaves.
7. Drizzle with olive oil and sprinkle with salt to taste before serving.

Pepperoni Pizza

Ingredients:

- 1 pizza dough
- 1/2 cup pizza sauce
- 8 oz mozzarella cheese, shredded
- 3 oz pepperoni slices

Instructions:

1. Preheat the oven to 475°F (245°C).
2. Roll out the pizza dough and transfer it to a baking sheet or pizza stone.
3. Spread the pizza sauce evenly on the dough.
4. Sprinkle shredded mozzarella cheese over the sauce.
5. Arrange the pepperoni slices evenly on top.
6. Bake for 10-12 minutes until the crust is golden and the cheese is bubbly.
7. Slice and serve hot.

Quattro Stagioni Pizza

Ingredients:

- 1 pizza dough
- 1/2 cup tomato sauce
- 8 oz mozzarella cheese, shredded
- 2 oz artichoke hearts, quartered
- 2 oz black olives, pitted and sliced
- 2 oz ham, thinly sliced
- 2 oz mushrooms, sliced
- Olive oil

Instructions:

1. Preheat the oven to 475°F (245°C).
2. Roll out the pizza dough and place it on a baking sheet or pizza stone.
3. Spread the tomato sauce on the dough.
4. Sprinkle shredded mozzarella cheese on top.
5. Arrange the artichokes, olives, ham, and mushrooms in four sections, one for each "season."
6. Bake for 10-12 minutes until the crust is golden and cheese is melted.
7. Drizzle with olive oil before serving.

BBQ Chicken Pizza

Ingredients:

- 1 pizza dough
- 1/2 cup BBQ sauce
- 8 oz cooked chicken breast, shredded
- 1/2 red onion, thinly sliced
- 8 oz mozzarella cheese, shredded
- Fresh cilantro for garnish

Instructions:

1. Preheat the oven to 475°F (245°C).
2. Roll out the pizza dough and transfer it to a baking sheet or pizza stone.
3. Spread BBQ sauce evenly over the dough.
4. Top with shredded chicken, red onion, and mozzarella cheese.
5. Bake for 10-12 minutes until the crust is golden and the cheese is bubbly.
6. Garnish with fresh cilantro before serving.

Prosciutto and Arugula Pizza

Ingredients:

- 1 pizza dough
- 1/2 cup tomato sauce
- 8 oz mozzarella cheese, shredded
- 4 oz prosciutto, thinly sliced
- 1 cup fresh arugula
- Olive oil

Instructions:

1. Preheat the oven to 475°F (245°C).
2. Roll out the pizza dough and place it on a baking sheet or pizza stone.
3. Spread tomato sauce on the dough and top with shredded mozzarella cheese.
4. Bake for 10-12 minutes until the crust is golden and the cheese is melted.
5. Remove the pizza from the oven and arrange prosciutto slices and fresh arugula on top.
6. Drizzle with olive oil before serving.

Veggie Supreme Pizza

Ingredients:

- 1 pizza dough
- 1/2 cup tomato sauce
- 8 oz mozzarella cheese, shredded
- 1/2 bell pepper, thinly sliced
- 1/2 red onion, thinly sliced
- 1/2 zucchini, thinly sliced
- 4 oz mushrooms, sliced
- 1/2 cup spinach leaves

Instructions:

1. Preheat the oven to 475°F (245°C).
2. Roll out the pizza dough and transfer it to a baking sheet or pizza stone.
3. Spread tomato sauce on the dough and top with shredded mozzarella cheese.
4. Arrange the bell pepper, onion, zucchini, mushrooms, and spinach on top.
5. Bake for 10-12 minutes until the crust is golden and the cheese is melted.
6. Slice and serve.

Hawaiian Pizza

Ingredients:

- 1 pizza dough
- 1/2 cup pizza sauce
- 8 oz mozzarella cheese, shredded
- 1 cup pineapple chunks
- 4 oz ham, diced

Instructions:

1. Preheat the oven to 475°F (245°C).
2. Roll out the pizza dough and place it on a baking sheet or pizza stone.
3. Spread pizza sauce on the dough and sprinkle with shredded mozzarella cheese.
4. Top with pineapple chunks and diced ham.
5. Bake for 10-12 minutes until the crust is golden and the cheese is bubbly.
6. Slice and serve.

White Garlic Chicken Pizza

Ingredients:

- 1 pizza dough
- 1/2 cup Alfredo sauce
- 8 oz cooked chicken breast, shredded
- 1/4 cup garlic, minced
- 8 oz mozzarella cheese, shredded
- Fresh parsley for garnish

Instructions:

1. Preheat the oven to 475°F (245°C).
2. Roll out the pizza dough and transfer it to a baking sheet or pizza stone.
3. Spread Alfredo sauce over the dough and top with shredded chicken.
4. Sprinkle minced garlic and shredded mozzarella cheese on top.
5. Bake for 10-12 minutes until the crust is golden and the cheese is melted.
6. Garnish with fresh parsley before serving.

Margherita with Balsamic Glaze

Ingredients:

- 1 pizza dough
- 1/2 cup tomato sauce
- 8 oz fresh mozzarella cheese, sliced
- Fresh basil leaves
- Balsamic glaze for drizzling

Instructions:

1. Preheat the oven to 475°F (245°C).
2. Roll out the pizza dough and place it on a baking sheet or pizza stone.
3. Spread tomato sauce on the dough and top with fresh mozzarella cheese slices.
4. Bake for 10-12 minutes until the crust is golden and the cheese is melted.
5. Remove from the oven and top with fresh basil leaves.
6. Drizzle with balsamic glaze before serving.

Spicy Italian Sausage Pizza

Ingredients:

- 1 pizza dough
- 1/2 cup pizza sauce
- 8 oz mozzarella cheese, shredded
- 4 oz spicy Italian sausage, cooked and crumbled
- 1/4 teaspoon red pepper flakes (optional)
- Fresh basil for garnish

Instructions:

1. Preheat the oven to 475°F (245°C).
2. Roll out the pizza dough and transfer it to a baking sheet or pizza stone.
3. Spread pizza sauce on the dough and top with shredded mozzarella cheese.
4. Sprinkle cooked and crumbled Italian sausage and red pepper flakes on top.
5. Bake for 10-12 minutes until the crust is golden and the cheese is bubbly.

Mushroom and Truffle Oil Pizza

Ingredients:

- 1 pizza dough
- 1/2 cup cream sauce or white sauce
- 8 oz mushrooms, sliced
- 8 oz mozzarella cheese, shredded
- 1 tablespoon truffle oil
- Fresh thyme or parsley for garnish
- Salt and pepper to taste

Instructions:

1. Preheat the oven to 475°F (245°C).
2. Roll out the pizza dough and transfer it to a baking sheet or pizza stone.
3. Spread the cream sauce evenly on the dough.
4. Top with sliced mushrooms and shredded mozzarella cheese.
5. Bake for 10-12 minutes until the crust is golden and the cheese is melted.
6. Drizzle with truffle oil, season with salt and pepper, and garnish with fresh thyme or parsley before serving.

Four Cheese Pizza (Quattro Formaggi)

Ingredients:

- 1 pizza dough
- 1/2 cup tomato sauce
- 4 oz mozzarella cheese, shredded
- 2 oz gorgonzola cheese, crumbled
- 2 oz ricotta cheese
- 2 oz parmesan cheese, grated
- Olive oil for drizzling

Instructions:

1. Preheat the oven to 475°F (245°C).
2. Roll out the pizza dough and place it on a baking sheet or pizza stone.
3. Spread tomato sauce evenly over the dough.
4. Sprinkle the mozzarella, gorgonzola, ricotta, and parmesan cheeses on top.
5. Bake for 10-12 minutes until the crust is golden and the cheeses are melted and bubbly.
6. Drizzle with olive oil before serving.

Shrimp Scampi Pizza

Ingredients:

- 1 pizza dough
- 1/2 cup garlic butter sauce (or Alfredo sauce)
- 8 oz shrimp, peeled and deveined
- 8 oz mozzarella cheese, shredded
- Fresh parsley for garnish
- Red pepper flakes (optional)

Instructions:

1. Preheat the oven to 475°F (245°C).
2. Roll out the pizza dough and transfer it to a baking sheet or pizza stone.
3. Spread garlic butter sauce evenly over the dough.
4. Arrange shrimp on top, followed by shredded mozzarella cheese.
5. Bake for 10-12 minutes until the crust is golden and the cheese is melted.
6. Garnish with fresh parsley and red pepper flakes if desired before serving.

Pesto Chicken Pizza

Ingredients:

- 1 pizza dough
- 1/2 cup pesto sauce
- 8 oz cooked chicken breast, shredded
- 8 oz mozzarella cheese, shredded
- Cherry tomatoes, halved
- Fresh basil for garnish

Instructions:

1. Preheat the oven to 475°F (245°C).
2. Roll out the pizza dough and place it on a baking sheet or pizza stone.
3. Spread pesto sauce evenly over the dough.
4. Top with shredded chicken, mozzarella cheese, and halved cherry tomatoes.
5. Bake for 10-12 minutes until the crust is golden and the cheese is melted.
6. Garnish with fresh basil leaves before serving.

Buffalo Chicken Pizza

Ingredients:

- 1 pizza dough
- 1/2 cup buffalo sauce
- 8 oz cooked chicken breast, shredded
- 8 oz mozzarella cheese, shredded
- Blue cheese crumbles
- Celery, thinly sliced (for garnish)

Instructions:

1. Preheat the oven to 475°F (245°C).
2. Roll out the pizza dough and transfer it to a baking sheet or pizza stone.
3. Spread buffalo sauce evenly over the dough.
4. Top with shredded chicken, mozzarella cheese, and blue cheese crumbles.
5. Bake for 10-12 minutes until the crust is golden and the cheese is melted.
6. Garnish with thinly sliced celery before serving.

Fig and Prosciutto Pizza

Ingredients:

- 1 pizza dough
- 1/2 cup balsamic glaze
- 8 oz mozzarella cheese, shredded
- 4 oz prosciutto, thinly sliced
- 4 figs, sliced
- Fresh arugula for garnish

Instructions:

1. Preheat the oven to 475°F (245°C).
2. Roll out the pizza dough and place it on a baking sheet or pizza stone.
3. Spread balsamic glaze evenly over the dough.
4. Top with shredded mozzarella cheese, prosciutto, and fig slices.
5. Bake for 10-12 minutes until the crust is golden and the cheese is melted.
6. Garnish with fresh arugula before serving.

Spinach and Ricotta Pizza

Ingredients:

- 1 pizza dough
- 1/2 cup tomato sauce
- 8 oz mozzarella cheese, shredded
- 1/2 cup ricotta cheese
- 1 cup fresh spinach leaves
- Olive oil for drizzling

Instructions:

1. Preheat the oven to 475°F (245°C).
2. Roll out the pizza dough and transfer it to a baking sheet or pizza stone.
3. Spread tomato sauce evenly over the dough.
4. Sprinkle shredded mozzarella cheese, ricotta cheese, and fresh spinach on top.
5. Bake for 10-12 minutes until the crust is golden and the cheese is melted.
6. Drizzle with olive oil before serving.

Meat Lovers Pizza

Ingredients:

- 1 pizza dough
- 1/2 cup pizza sauce
- 8 oz mozzarella cheese, shredded
- 4 oz pepperoni, sliced
- 4 oz cooked sausage, crumbled
- 4 oz cooked bacon, crumbled
- 4 oz cooked ham, diced

Instructions:

1. Preheat the oven to 475°F (245°C).
2. Roll out the pizza dough and transfer it to a baking sheet or pizza stone.
3. Spread pizza sauce evenly over the dough.
4. Sprinkle shredded mozzarella cheese and layer with pepperoni, sausage, bacon, and ham.
5. Bake for 10-12 minutes until the crust is golden and the cheese is bubbly.
6. Slice and serve.

Caprese Pizza

Ingredients:

- 1 pizza dough
- 1/2 cup tomato sauce
- 8 oz fresh mozzarella cheese, sliced
- 1 cup cherry tomatoes, halved
- Fresh basil leaves
- Olive oil for drizzling
- Balsamic glaze for drizzling

Instructions:

1. Preheat the oven to 475°F (245°C).
2. Roll out the pizza dough and place it on a baking sheet or pizza stone.
3. Spread tomato sauce evenly over the dough.
4. Top with fresh mozzarella cheese slices and halved cherry tomatoes.
5. Bake for 10-12 minutes until the crust is golden and the cheese is melted.
6. Garnish with fresh basil leaves and drizzle with olive oil and balsamic glaze before serving.

Eggplant Parmesan Pizza

Ingredients:

- 1 pizza dough
- 1/2 cup tomato sauce
- 8 oz mozzarella cheese, shredded
- 8 oz eggplant, sliced and roasted
- 2 oz parmesan cheese, grated
- Fresh basil for garnish

Instructions:

1. Preheat the oven to 475°F (245°C).
2. Roll out the pizza dough and transfer it to a baking sheet or pizza stone.
3. Spread tomato sauce evenly over the dough.
4. Layer with shredded mozzarella, roasted eggplant slices, and parmesan cheese.
5. Bake for 10-12 minutes until the crust is golden and the cheese is melted.
6. Garnish with fresh basil before serving.
6. Garnish with fresh basil leaves before serving.

Clam Pizza

Ingredients:

- 1 pizza dough
- 1/2 cup white sauce (or garlic butter sauce)
- 1/2 cup mozzarella cheese, shredded
- 8 oz canned clams, drained
- 2 cloves garlic, minced
- Fresh parsley, chopped
- Lemon wedges for garnish
- Salt and pepper to taste

Instructions:

1. Preheat the oven to 475°F (245°C).
2. Roll out the pizza dough and transfer it to a baking sheet or pizza stone.
3. Spread the white sauce evenly over the dough.
4. Sprinkle with shredded mozzarella cheese, followed by clams, minced garlic, and a pinch of salt and pepper.
5. Bake for 10-12 minutes until the crust is golden and the cheese is melted.
6. Garnish with fresh parsley and serve with lemon wedges.

Roasted Red Pepper and Goat Cheese Pizza

Ingredients:

- 1 pizza dough
- 1/2 cup tomato sauce
- 8 oz goat cheese, crumbled
- 1/2 cup roasted red peppers, sliced
- Fresh basil leaves for garnish
- Olive oil for drizzling

Instructions:

1. Preheat the oven to 475°F (245°C).
2. Roll out the pizza dough and place it on a baking sheet or pizza stone.
3. Spread tomato sauce evenly over the dough.
4. Top with crumbled goat cheese and sliced roasted red peppers.
5. Bake for 10-12 minutes until the crust is golden and the cheese is melted.
6. Drizzle with olive oil and garnish with fresh basil before serving.

Sausage and Peppers Pizza

Ingredients:

- 1 pizza dough
- 1/2 cup pizza sauce
- 8 oz mozzarella cheese, shredded
- 4 oz Italian sausage, cooked and crumbled
- 1/2 cup bell peppers, sliced
- 1/2 cup onions, sliced
- Olive oil for drizzling

Instructions:

1. Preheat the oven to 475°F (245°C).
2. Roll out the pizza dough and transfer it to a baking sheet or pizza stone.
3. Spread pizza sauce evenly over the dough.
4. Sprinkle with mozzarella cheese and top with crumbled sausage, sliced peppers, and onions.
5. Bake for 10-12 minutes until the crust is golden and the cheese is melted.
6. Drizzle with olive oil and serve.

Mediterranean Pizza (Olives, Feta, and Spinach)

Ingredients:

- 1 pizza dough
- 1/2 cup tomato sauce
- 8 oz mozzarella cheese, shredded
- 1/2 cup feta cheese, crumbled
- 1/2 cup Kalamata olives, sliced
- 1 cup fresh spinach leaves
- Fresh oregano for garnish

Instructions:

1. Preheat the oven to 475°F (245°C).
2. Roll out the pizza dough and place it on a baking sheet or pizza stone.
3. Spread tomato sauce evenly over the dough.
4. Top with mozzarella cheese, feta cheese, olives, and fresh spinach.
5. Bake for 10-12 minutes until the crust is golden and the cheese is melted.
6. Garnish with fresh oregano before serving.

Mexican Street Corn Pizza

Ingredients:

- 1 pizza dough
- 1/2 cup sour cream
- 1/2 cup mozzarella cheese, shredded
- 1 cup corn kernels, roasted or grilled
- 1/4 cup cotija cheese, crumbled
- 1/2 teaspoon chili powder
- Fresh cilantro for garnish
- Lime wedges for serving

Instructions:

1. Preheat the oven to 475°F (245°C).
2. Roll out the pizza dough and transfer it to a baking sheet or pizza stone.
3. Spread sour cream evenly over the dough.
4. Sprinkle with shredded mozzarella cheese, roasted corn, and cotija cheese.
5. Bake for 10-12 minutes until the crust is golden and the cheese is melted.
6. Garnish with chili powder and fresh cilantro.
7. Serve with lime wedges.

BBQ Pulled Pork Pizza

Ingredients:

- 1 pizza dough
- 1/2 cup BBQ sauce
- 8 oz mozzarella cheese, shredded
- 1 cup pulled pork
- 1/2 red onion, thinly sliced
- Fresh cilantro for garnish

Instructions:

1. Preheat the oven to 475°F (245°C).
2. Roll out the pizza dough and place it on a baking sheet or pizza stone.
3. Spread BBQ sauce evenly over the dough.
4. Top with shredded mozzarella, pulled pork, and thinly sliced red onion.
5. Bake for 10-12 minutes until the crust is golden and the cheese is melted.
6. Garnish with fresh cilantro before serving.

Smoked Salmon and Cream Cheese Pizza

Ingredients:

- 1 pizza dough
- 1/2 cup cream cheese, softened
- 8 oz smoked salmon, sliced
- 1/2 red onion, thinly sliced
- Fresh dill for garnish
- Lemon wedges for serving

Instructions:

1. Preheat the oven to 475°F (245°C).
2. Roll out the pizza dough and transfer it to a baking sheet or pizza stone.
3. Spread cream cheese evenly over the dough.
4. Top with smoked salmon slices, red onion, and a drizzle of olive oil.
5. Bake for 8-10 minutes until the crust is golden and the cream cheese is slightly set.
6. Garnish with fresh dill and serve with lemon wedges.

Breakfast Pizza (Eggs and Bacon)

Ingredients:

- 1 pizza dough
- 1/2 cup pizza sauce or olive oil
- 8 oz mozzarella cheese, shredded
- 4 strips bacon, cooked and crumbled
- 2 eggs
- Fresh parsley for garnish

Instructions:

1. Preheat the oven to 475°F (245°C).
2. Roll out the pizza dough and place it on a baking sheet or pizza stone.
3. Spread olive oil or pizza sauce evenly over the dough.
4. Sprinkle with shredded mozzarella cheese and crumbled bacon.
5. Crack the eggs onto the pizza, being careful not to break the yolks.
6. Bake for 10-12 minutes until the crust is golden, the cheese is melted, and the eggs are cooked to your liking.
7. Garnish with fresh parsley before serving.

Beef and Blue Cheese Pizza

Ingredients:

- 1 pizza dough
- 1/2 cup pizza sauce
- 8 oz mozzarella cheese, shredded
- 4 oz cooked beef, thinly sliced (e.g., steak or roast beef)
- 2 oz blue cheese, crumbled
- Fresh arugula for garnish

Instructions:

1. Preheat the oven to 475°F (245°C).
2. Roll out the pizza dough and transfer it to a baking sheet or pizza stone.
3. Spread pizza sauce evenly over the dough.
4. Top with shredded mozzarella, thinly sliced beef, and crumbled blue cheese.
5. Bake for 10-12 minutes until the crust is golden and the cheese is melted.
6. Garnish with fresh arugula before serving.

Peppadew and Ricotta Pizza

Ingredients:

- 1 pizza dough
- 1/2 cup tomato sauce
- 8 oz mozzarella cheese, shredded
- 4 oz peppadew peppers, sliced
- 1/2 cup ricotta cheese
- Fresh basil for garnish

Instructions:

1. Preheat the oven to 475°F (245°C).
2. Roll out the pizza dough and place it on a baking sheet or pizza stone.
3. Spread tomato sauce evenly over the dough.
4. Sprinkle with shredded mozzarella, sliced peppadew peppers, and dollops of ricotta cheese.
5. Bake for 10-12 minutes until the crust is golden and the cheese is melted.
6. Garnish with fresh basil before serving.

Pear and Gorgonzola Pizza

Ingredients:

- 1 pizza dough
- 1/2 cup olive oil or white sauce
- 1/2 cup mozzarella cheese, shredded
- 1/2 cup Gorgonzola cheese, crumbled
- 2 pears, thinly sliced
- Walnuts, chopped (optional)
- Fresh arugula for garnish

Instructions:

1. Preheat the oven to 475°F (245°C).
2. Roll out the pizza dough and transfer it to a baking sheet or pizza stone.
3. Spread olive oil or white sauce evenly over the dough.
4. Sprinkle with shredded mozzarella, crumbled Gorgonzola, and thinly sliced pears.
5. Add walnuts on top if using.
6. Bake for 10-12 minutes until the crust is golden and the cheese is melted.
7. Garnish with fresh arugula before serving.

Mushroom and Bacon Pizza

Ingredients:

- 1 pizza dough
- 1/2 cup pizza sauce
- 1/2 cup mozzarella cheese, shredded
- 1/2 cup mushrooms, sliced
- 4 strips bacon, cooked and crumbled
- Fresh thyme for garnish

Instructions:

1. Preheat the oven to 475°F (245°C).
2. Roll out the pizza dough and place it on a baking sheet or pizza stone.
3. Spread pizza sauce evenly over the dough.
4. Sprinkle with shredded mozzarella, followed by sliced mushrooms and crumbled bacon.
5. Bake for 10-12 minutes until the crust is golden and the cheese is melted.
6. Garnish with fresh thyme before serving.

Chicken Alfredo Pizza

Ingredients:

- 1 pizza dough
- 1/2 cup Alfredo sauce
- 1/2 cup mozzarella cheese, shredded
- 1 cup cooked chicken breast, sliced
- 1/4 cup Parmesan cheese, grated
- Fresh parsley for garnish

Instructions:

1. Preheat the oven to 475°F (245°C).
2. Roll out the pizza dough and transfer it to a baking sheet or pizza stone.
3. Spread Alfredo sauce evenly over the dough.
4. Top with shredded mozzarella, sliced chicken, and grated Parmesan cheese.
5. Bake for 10-12 minutes until the crust is golden and the cheese is melted.
6. Garnish with fresh parsley before serving.

Zaatar and Feta Pizza

Ingredients:

- 1 pizza dough
- 2 tablespoons olive oil
- 1 tablespoon zaatar spice mix
- 1/2 cup feta cheese, crumbled
- Fresh parsley for garnish

Instructions:

1. Preheat the oven to 475°F (245°C).
2. Roll out the pizza dough and transfer it to a baking sheet or pizza stone.
3. Drizzle olive oil over the dough and sprinkle with zaatar spice mix.
4. Sprinkle with crumbled feta cheese.
5. Bake for 10-12 minutes until the crust is golden and the cheese is melted.
6. Garnish with fresh parsley before serving.

Black Olive and Anchovy Pizza

Ingredients:

- 1 pizza dough
- 1/2 cup tomato sauce
- 1/2 cup mozzarella cheese, shredded
- 1/4 cup black olives, sliced
- 8-10 anchovy fillets, drained
- Fresh oregano for garnish

Instructions:

1. Preheat the oven to 475°F (245°C).
2. Roll out the pizza dough and place it on a baking sheet or pizza stone.
3. Spread tomato sauce evenly over the dough.
4. Sprinkle with shredded mozzarella, sliced black olives, and anchovy fillets.
5. Bake for 10-12 minutes until the crust is golden and the cheese is melted.
6. Garnish with fresh oregano before serving.

White Pizzaiola (Tomato-Free Pizza)

Ingredients:

- 1 pizza dough
- 1/2 cup ricotta cheese
- 1/2 cup mozzarella cheese, shredded
- 1/4 cup Parmesan cheese, grated
- 2 cloves garlic, minced
- Fresh rosemary for garnish

Instructions:

1. Preheat the oven to 475°F (245°C).
2. Roll out the pizza dough and transfer it to a baking sheet or pizza stone.
3. Spread ricotta cheese evenly over the dough.
4. Top with shredded mozzarella, grated Parmesan, and minced garlic.
5. Bake for 10-12 minutes until the crust is golden and the cheese is melted.
6. Garnish with fresh rosemary before serving.

Spicy Tuna Pizza

Ingredients:

- 1 pizza dough
- 1/2 cup tomato sauce
- 1/2 cup mozzarella cheese, shredded
- 1 can tuna, drained and flaked
- 1/4 teaspoon chili flakes
- Fresh cilantro for garnish

Instructions:

1. Preheat the oven to 475°F (245°C).
2. Roll out the pizza dough and place it on a baking sheet or pizza stone.
3. Spread tomato sauce evenly over the dough.
4. Top with shredded mozzarella, flaked tuna, and chili flakes.
5. Bake for 10-12 minutes until the crust is golden and the cheese is melted.
6. Garnish with fresh cilantro before serving.

Margherita with Burrata

Ingredients:

- 1 pizza dough
- 1/2 cup tomato sauce
- 1/2 cup mozzarella cheese, shredded
- 1 ball burrata cheese
- Fresh basil leaves
- Olive oil for drizzling

Instructions:

1. Preheat the oven to 475°F (245°C).
2. Roll out the pizza dough and transfer it to a baking sheet or pizza stone.
3. Spread tomato sauce evenly over the dough.
4. Sprinkle with shredded mozzarella cheese.
5. Bake for 10-12 minutes until the crust is golden and the cheese is melted.
6. Once out of the oven, place the burrata cheese on top and drizzle with olive oil.
7. Garnish with fresh basil leaves before serving.

Shrimp and Pesto Pizza

Ingredients:

- 1 pizza dough
- 1/2 cup pesto sauce
- 1/2 cup mozzarella cheese, shredded
- 1/2 pound cooked shrimp, peeled and deveined
- Fresh arugula for garnish

Instructions:

1. Preheat the oven to 475°F (245°C).
2. Roll out the pizza dough and place it on a baking sheet or pizza stone.
3. Spread pesto sauce evenly over the dough.
4. Top with shredded mozzarella and cooked shrimp.
5. Bake for 10-12 minutes until the crust is golden and the cheese is melted.
6. Garnish with fresh arugula before serving.

Caramelized Onion and Goat Cheese Pizza

Ingredients:

- 1 pizza dough
- 1 tablespoon olive oil
- 2 large onions, thinly sliced
- 1/2 cup goat cheese, crumbled
- 1/2 cup mozzarella cheese, shredded
- 1 tablespoon balsamic vinegar
- Fresh thyme for garnish

Instructions:

1. Preheat the oven to 475°F (245°C).
2. In a skillet, heat olive oil over medium heat. Add onions and cook, stirring occasionally, for 15-20 minutes until caramelized. Add balsamic vinegar and stir to combine.
3. Roll out the pizza dough and transfer it to a baking sheet or pizza stone.
4. Spread the caramelized onions evenly over the dough.
5. Sprinkle with goat cheese and shredded mozzarella.
6. Bake for 10-12 minutes until the crust is golden and the cheese is melted.
7. Garnish with fresh thyme before serving.

Artichoke and Parmesan Pizza

Ingredients:

- 1 pizza dough
- 1/2 cup mozzarella cheese, shredded
- 1/2 cup Parmesan cheese, grated
- 1 can artichoke hearts, drained and chopped
- 2 cloves garlic, minced
- Fresh parsley for garnish

Instructions:

1. Preheat the oven to 475°F (245°C).
2. Roll out the pizza dough and transfer it to a baking sheet or pizza stone.
3. Sprinkle the shredded mozzarella and grated Parmesan over the dough.
4. Scatter the chopped artichokes and minced garlic on top.
5. Bake for 10-12 minutes until the crust is golden and the cheese is melted.
6. Garnish with fresh parsley before serving.

Chorizo and Sweet Potato Pizza

Ingredients:

- 1 pizza dough
- 1/2 cup tomato sauce
- 1/2 cup mozzarella cheese, shredded
- 1/2 cup cooked chorizo, crumbled
- 1 small sweet potato, peeled and thinly sliced
- Fresh cilantro for garnish

Instructions:

1. Preheat the oven to 475°F (245°C).
2. Roll out the pizza dough and transfer it to a baking sheet or pizza stone.
3. Spread tomato sauce evenly over the dough.
4. Sprinkle with shredded mozzarella, followed by crumbled chorizo and sweet potato slices.
5. Bake for 10-12 minutes until the crust is golden and the cheese is melted.
6. Garnish with fresh cilantro before serving.

Bacon and Brussels Sprouts Pizza

Ingredients:

- 1 pizza dough
- 1/2 cup mozzarella cheese, shredded
- 1/4 cup Parmesan cheese, grated
- 4 slices bacon, cooked and crumbled
- 1 cup Brussels sprouts, thinly sliced
- Olive oil for drizzling

Instructions:

1. Preheat the oven to 475°F (245°C).
2. Roll out the pizza dough and transfer it to a baking sheet or pizza stone.
3. Sprinkle the shredded mozzarella and grated Parmesan over the dough.
4. Top with crumbled bacon and sliced Brussels sprouts.
5. Drizzle with olive oil and bake for 10-12 minutes until the crust is golden and the cheese is melted.
6. Garnish with additional Parmesan if desired before serving.

Italian Sausage and Ricotta Pizza

Ingredients:

- 1 pizza dough
- 1/2 cup tomato sauce
- 1/2 cup mozzarella cheese, shredded
- 1/2 cup ricotta cheese
- 1/2 cup Italian sausage, cooked and crumbled
- Fresh basil leaves for garnish

Instructions:

1. Preheat the oven to 475°F (245°C).
2. Roll out the pizza dough and transfer it to a baking sheet or pizza stone.
3. Spread tomato sauce evenly over the dough.
4. Sprinkle with shredded mozzarella, followed by dollops of ricotta cheese and crumbled Italian sausage.
5. Bake for 10-12 minutes until the crust is golden and the cheese is melted.
6. Garnish with fresh basil leaves before serving.

Roasted Beet and Arugula Pizza

Ingredients:

- 1 pizza dough
- 2 medium beets, peeled and thinly sliced
- 1 tablespoon olive oil
- 1/2 cup mozzarella cheese, shredded
- 1/2 cup goat cheese, crumbled
- 1 cup fresh arugula
- Balsamic glaze for drizzling

Instructions:

1. Preheat the oven to 475°F (245°C).
2. Toss the beet slices with olive oil, salt, and pepper, and spread them on a baking sheet. Roast for 25-30 minutes until tender.
3. Roll out the pizza dough and transfer it to a baking sheet or pizza stone.
4. Sprinkle shredded mozzarella over the dough, then top with roasted beets and crumbled goat cheese.
5. Bake for 10-12 minutes until the crust is golden and the cheese is melted.
6. Remove from the oven, top with fresh arugula, and drizzle with balsamic glaze before serving.

Wild Mushroom and Thyme Pizza

Ingredients:

- 1 pizza dough
- 2 cups mixed wild mushrooms, sliced
- 1 tablespoon olive oil
- 1/2 cup mozzarella cheese, shredded
- 1/4 cup Parmesan cheese, grated
- 1 teaspoon fresh thyme leaves
- 2 cloves garlic, minced
- Fresh parsley for garnish

Instructions:

1. Preheat the oven to 475°F (245°C).
2. In a skillet, heat olive oil over medium heat. Add garlic and wild mushrooms, and sauté for 5-7 minutes until softened. Season with thyme, salt, and pepper.
3. Roll out the pizza dough and transfer it to a baking sheet or pizza stone.
4. Sprinkle mozzarella and Parmesan over the dough, followed by the sautéed mushrooms and garlic.
5. Bake for 10-12 minutes until the crust is golden and the cheese is melted.
6. Garnish with fresh parsley before serving.

Roasted Garlic and Tomato Pizza

Ingredients:

- 1 pizza dough
- 1/2 cup tomato sauce
- 1/2 cup mozzarella cheese, shredded
- 2 heads garlic, roasted (see instructions)
- 1 cup cherry tomatoes, halved
- Fresh basil leaves for garnish

Instructions:

1. Preheat the oven to 475°F (245°C).
2. To roast the garlic, cut the top off the garlic heads, drizzle with olive oil, wrap in foil, and roast for 30-35 minutes until soft.
3. Roll out the pizza dough and transfer it to a baking sheet or pizza stone.
4. Spread tomato sauce evenly over the dough, then add shredded mozzarella and squeeze out the roasted garlic from the cloves.
5. Scatter cherry tomatoes over the pizza and bake for 10-12 minutes until the crust is golden and the cheese is melted.
6. Garnish with fresh basil leaves before serving.

Sweet and Sour Pork Pizza

Ingredients:

- 1 pizza dough
- 1/2 cup mozzarella cheese, shredded
- 1/2 cup cooked pork (leftover or ground), crumbled
- 1/4 cup pineapple chunks
- 2 tablespoons sweet and sour sauce
- Red onion, thinly sliced
- Fresh cilantro for garnish

Instructions:

1. Preheat the oven to 475°F (245°C).
2. Roll out the pizza dough and transfer it to a baking sheet or pizza stone.
3. Spread mozzarella cheese over the dough, followed by cooked pork, pineapple chunks, and red onion slices.
4. Drizzle sweet and sour sauce over the top.
5. Bake for 10-12 minutes until the crust is golden and the cheese is melted.
6. Garnish with fresh cilantro before serving.

Butternut Squash and Sage Pizza

Ingredients:

- 1 pizza dough
- 1/2 cup mozzarella cheese, shredded
- 1 small butternut squash, peeled and cubed
- 1 tablespoon olive oil
- 1 tablespoon fresh sage, chopped
- 1/4 cup ricotta cheese
- Fresh thyme for garnish

Instructions:

1. Preheat the oven to 475°F (245°C).
2. Toss the butternut squash cubes with olive oil, salt, and pepper. Roast for 20-25 minutes until tender.
3. Roll out the pizza dough and transfer it to a baking sheet or pizza stone.
4. Spread mozzarella cheese over the dough, followed by roasted butternut squash, fresh sage, and dollops of ricotta cheese.
5. Bake for 10-12 minutes until the crust is golden and the cheese is melted.
6. Garnish with fresh thyme before serving.

Grilled Vegetable Pizza

Ingredients:

- 1 pizza dough
- 1/2 cup tomato sauce
- 1/2 cup mozzarella cheese, shredded
- 1 zucchini, thinly sliced
- 1 red bell pepper, sliced
- 1/2 red onion, sliced
- 1 tablespoon olive oil
- Fresh basil for garnish

Instructions:

1. Preheat the oven to 475°F (245°C).
2. Grill the zucchini, bell pepper, and onion slices on a grill pan or grill for 4-5 minutes until tender and charred.
3. Roll out the pizza dough and transfer it to a baking sheet or pizza stone.
4. Spread tomato sauce evenly over the dough, then sprinkle with mozzarella cheese.
5. Top with the grilled vegetables and bake for 10-12 minutes until the crust is golden and the cheese is melted.
6. Garnish with fresh basil before serving.